# A TREATISE
# ON THE PRACTICE OF
# MENSURAL MUSIC
# IN THE ITALIAN MANNER

MUSICOLOGICAL STUDIES & DOCUMENTS

29

PROSDOCIMUS DE BELDEMANDIS

# A TREATISE ON THE PRACTICE OF MENSURAL MUSIC IN THE ITALIAN MANNER

*(Tractatus practicae cantus mensurabilis ad modum Ytalicorum)*

Translated and edited by

JAY A. HUFF

AMERICAN INSTITUTE OF MUSICOLOGY

1972

# INTRODUCTION

The *Tractatus practicae cantus mensurabilis ad modum Ytalicorum* of Prosdocimus de Beldemandis exists in two redactions, each deriving from a single manuscript source. The first is contained in Ms. A 56 of the Civico Museo Bibliografico Musicale, Bologna, fol. $51^{r}$-$57^{r}$ (edition in C. E. H. de Coussemaker's *Scriptorum de musica medii aevi nova series*, III [Paris, 1869], pp. 228-248); the second, in Ms. 359 of the Biblioteca Governativa, Lucca, fol. $34^{r}$-$47^{r}$ (edition in Claudio Sartori's *La notazione italiana del Trecento in una redazione inedita del "Tractatus practice cantus mensurabilis ad modum ytalicorum" di Prosdocimo de Beldemandis* [Firenze, 1938], pp. 35-71). A description of these manuscripts along with a listing of their contents will be found in F. Alberto Gallo's article "La tradizione dei tratti musicali di Prosdocimo de Beldemandis," in *Quadrivium* VI (1964), pp. 57-82.

The present translation of the second redaction is based upon a collation of the manuscript copy with Sartori's edition. A list of *errata* in that edition follows.

| **Sartori** | | | **Bibl. Governativa Ms. 359** | | |
|---|---|---|---|---|---|
| Page | Line | | Folium | Line | |
| 35 | 16 | diminuita | $34^{r}$ | 35 | diminuta |
| 37 | 19 | quomodo | $34^{v}$ | 58 | quoniam |
| 37 | 25 | figarum | $34^{v}$ | 69 | figurarum |
| 39 | 8 | cantu | $35^{v}$ | 27 | cantus |
| 39 | 16 | perperfigurationem | $35^{v}$ | 42 | patet per figurationem |
| 39 | 18 | pro | $35^{v}$ | 48 | patet |
| 39 | *With reference to f.n. (5), the codex has:* | | $35^{v}$ | 63 | valore |
| 42 | 4 | quomodo | $36^{v}$ | 53 | qualiter |
| 42 | 9 | tantum | $36^{v}$ | 63 | tamen |
| 44 | 7 | propter quod | $37^{v}$ | 42-43 | preterea quia |
| 44 | 10 | pro | $37^{v}$ | 49 | patet |

| | | | | | |
|---|---|---|---|---|---|
| 44 | 35 | si | 38ʳ | 11 | nisi |
| 44 | *With reference to f.n. (7), the codex has:* | | 37ᵛ | 67 | perfectam |
| 45 | 11 | niso | 38ʳ | 30 | nisi |
| 45 | 15 | quare | 38ʳ | 36 | quia |
| 45 | 26 & 28 | puct-(o,i) | 38ʳ | 56 & 61 | punct-(o,i) |
| 46 | 32 | sina | 38ᵛ | 54 | sine |
| 46 | *With reference to f.n. (9), the codex has:* | | 38ᵛ | 33-34 | non in perfectione |
| 47 | 14 & 15 | quidam | 39ʳ | 4 | quedam |
| 47 | 30 | Item pro modo longarum | 39ʳ | 29-30 | Pro modo vero longarum |
| 47 | 31 | NL et P | 39ʳ | 31 | N et L et P |
| 47 | 32 | pro imperfecto longarum | 39ʳ | 33 | et pro imperfecto modo longarum |
| 48 | 10 | he | 39ʳ | 57 | hec |
| 48 | 32 | necessarium | 39ᵛ | 18 | necessariam |
| 49 | 4 | obstaret | 39ᵛ | 36 | instaret |
| 51 | 24 | recte | 40ᵛ | 14 | directe |
| 52 | 17 | pro Aristotiles | 40ᵛ | 64 | per Aristotilem |
| 52 | 35 | sit | 41ʳ | 9 | fit |
| 53 | *With reference to f.n. (13) and (14), the examples are correct in the codex.* | | 41ʳ | 17 & 32 | |
| 56 | 29 | tempus | 42ʳ | 50 | temporis |
| 57 | *Ex. 2: the fourth punctus is not in the codex.* | | 42ᵛ | *post* 40 | |
| 63 | 2 |  | 44ᵛ | 66-67 |  |
| 64 | 6 | fuit | 45ʳ | 42 | fit |
| 64 | 17 | divisas | 45ʳ | 63 | diversas |
| 65 | (Ex. 1) |  | 45ᵛ | *post* 25 |  |
| 65 | (Ex. 4) |  | 45ᵛ | *post* 25 |  |

| | | | | | |
|---|---|---|---|---|---|
| 65 | 15 | in arte | $45^v$ | 61 | in hac arte |
| 65 | 17 | est | $45^v$ | 64 | et |
| 65 | 21 | debet etiam | $45^v$ | 70-71 | etiam debet |
| 66 | 7 | pausationem oppositam | $46^r$ | 3-4 | pausationes oppositarum |
| 66 | 28 | est descendens eius | $46^r$ | 40-41 | est eius |
| 67 | 26 | un | $46^v$ | 15 | ut |
| 67 | 26 |  | $46^v$ | 15 |  |
| 68 | 16 | perfecto | $46^v$ | 61 | imperfecto |
| 68 | 20 | perfecta | $46^v$ | 68 | perfecte |
| 68 | 22-23 | pertractandum | $46^v$ | 72-73 | perscrutandum |
| 69 | 30 | nominantur | $47^v$ | 4 | nominatur |
| 69 | 32 | sacra dans | $47^v$ | 7 | dans sacra |
| 69 | 33 | duobus diversis respectibus | $47^v$ | 9-11 | duobus diversis nominibus scilicet color et talea dato quod diversis respectibus |
| 70 | 2 | huiuscemodi | $47^v$ | 20-21 | huiusmodi |
| 70 | 7 | [et] sibi immediata | $47^v$ | 31 | [et aliam] sibi immediatam |
| 70 | 34 | habet | $48^r$ | 6 | habeat |
| 71 | 4 | discrepatia | $48^r$ | 14 | discrepantia |
| 71 | 11 | Al | $48^r$ | 29 | ad |

To the corrections of the text made by Sartori the following may be added:

| *datis* | Sart. | Ms. | *intellege* |
|---|---|---|---|
| minorem | 36,20 | $34^v$,4 | minimam |
| ante brevem in tempore | 52,5 | $40^v$,43 | ante brevem vel eius pausam in tempore |
| in cantu senario | 52,12 | $40^v$,55 | in cantu de senario |
|  | (67,26)* | $46^v$,15 |  |

* For Sartori's version see above.

| | | | |
|---|---|---|---|
| ponenda semibrevis | 68,19 | 46$^{v}$,67-68 | ponenda pausa semibrevis |

In the notes that accompany the present translation no attempt has been made to deal analytically with the content of the treatise. This ground is covered thoroughly in Sartori's study (*op. cit.*, esp. ch. 3), and the reader is accordingly referred to that source. Information on mensural music in general, as well as on the various aspects of the Italian practice therein, is available from any one of several modern works on mensural notation. The two following are those cited in the notes: W. Apel, *The Notation of Polyphonic Music 900-1600*, 5th ed., Cambridge, 1953; J. Wolf, *Geschichte der Mensuralnotation von 1250-1460*, Vol. I, Leipzig, 1904.* (These and the other works already mentioned are hereafter referred to by surname of author only.) The notes, therefore, deal primarily with peripheral areas of the subject matter and with certain details of interpretation.

Subdivisions of the original text by subject titles, as found in many of the medieval treatises, are lacking in both versions of the present one. For ease of reference, therefore, these have been supplied here in square brackets, which are also used for parenthetical explanations within the text. In those instances in which the connection between an English word or phrase and its Latin equivalent might not be immediately obvious, the latter is placed in the text directly after the former and enclosed in parentheses.

For those who may be interested in a more extensive comparison of the Latin with the English, a few remarks on the general translation procedure and on the rendering of a few specific terms will be in order.

For the sake of a clearer explanation of the original (as well as for the sake of reasonably idiomatic English prose), the translation is more often interpretative than literal. However, Prosdocimus' style is generally quite straightforward and anyone with a modicum of acquaintance with Latin should have no difficulty in relating the

* A Prosdocimus bibliography by Heinrich Hüschen can be found in *Die Musik in Geschichte und Gegenwart* I, 1578-9.

translation to the original at any point. It has occasionally been necessary to resort to paraphrase and to fairly radical changes in syntactical structure, especially in instances of very long and complex sentences.

In the present context the terms *ars* and *practica* are virtually synonymous (Cf., e.g., the first sentence of the treatise, "Ars practicae ..." etc., where *practicae* is plainly an appositional genetive.) Either has approximately the force of the Greek τέχνη , that is, a set of procedural rules intended to enable anyone to operate effectively within a given discipline (cf. Sartori, p. 77). Both are usually translated here by the English cognate "practice," the other, "art," having extraneous connotations.

*Figurare*, "to notate mensurally," and *figuratio*, "mensural notation," are translated simply as "notate" and "notation" respectively, since in the context it is of course readily understood that such terms have to do only with mensural aspects of notation. *Figura*, the written symbol of a mensural value, is generally translated "note" or "note-form," as is *nota*. (Sartori asserts, p. 85, that *nota* is the sound itself whereas *figura* is the written symbol thereof; but it is plain that *nota*, like English "note," can stand for either. See, e.g., the second paragraph of the text.)

Except in the latter part of paragraph two (q.v.) where it is used in connection with plainchant to indicate something more or less like *tactus*, i.e., a fixed reference value, *mensura* in this treatise is the regular word for "mensuration" or "measure" — encompassing, that is, both "meter" and "measure," in modern terminology — and is translated either way, "mensuration" or "measure," according to which seems more appropriate in context.

*Mensura* thus replaces the term more usually found in expositions of the Italian practice, *divisio*, which in fact appears only once in the present treatise with this meaning (see note to p. 23). The verb form of the latter, *dividere*, like *mensurare*, can usually be understood as "determine," "fix," "distinguish," "mark," "measure," etc. (See, e.g., in Sartori, p. 39, par. 2: "Modus maximarum est mensura cuius perfectio et imperfectio ... mensurari sive dividi habet.")

In the original, as in much medieval Latin prose, conjunctions at the beginnings of sentences generally have no more literal significance than English "now" in the same position and are therefore sometimes translated contrary to their strict (dictionary) meanings — or not translated at all.

*Cantus* here, in its narrower sense, means "voice-part," while its broader meaning is simply "composition" or "piece of music." Since the distinction is rarely important, the latter more inclusive rendering is usually chosen.

Finally, the passive of *videre* frequently has the force, "be seen," "be apparant," "be obvious," rather than the classical "seem," "appear." Thus the combination *videtur quod* is often rendered as an adverb: "obviously," "plainly," "clearly," etc.

I wish to thank the librarian of the Biblioteca Governativa di Lucca for making a copy of the manuscript available to me, and express my gratitude to Dr. Richard H. Hoppin of The Ohio State University School of Music for several valuable suggestions pertaining to the interpretation of some problematical passages in the treatise.

J. A. H.

# A TREATISE ON THE PRACTICE OF MENSURAL MUSIC IN THE ITALIAN MANNER

The art or practice of mensural music is discovered to be of two kinds: There is the Italian practice, which at present only the Italians use, and there is the French practice, which all Europeans now embrace except the Italians. Of late, however, even the Italians have taken to using French practice — perhaps no less well than the French — and to such an extent that they are neglecting their own practice and reveling in the French, thinking their own defective and the French more elegant, more perfect, and more refined — the contrary of which view I shall present in what follows. Now, I believe this situation has come about simply because of the ignorance of present-day Italians, who do not know their own practice at all, though they think they do. I myself have made this mistake, with the result that at one time I expended a good deal of effort on the French practice, completing two works thereon, but when I looked into the Italian practice carefully, I decided at once that I had been seriously wrong in my former conviction, and at that point I resolved upon the composition of this treatise on the Italian practice of mensural music. I hope it will be accepted by those who are truly knowledgeable and that they will correct it, not out of malice but solely from good-will, by expanding whatever is too brief and abridging whatever is too prolix.

[The mensural notes]

Seeing, then, that mensural music, our present subject, is that in which the figures or notes are considered to have measure, i.e., that they are to be sung according to a species of measure determined by a note-form, this treatise must begin with the mensural notes. Consequently you should know that, among both the Italians and the French, there are six mensural notes in common use at the present time. To wit: the *maxima*, also called *duplex longa*, and written thus:  And it is named *maxima* because it has the maximum value of all the notes; it is called *duplex longa* because it sometimes has the value of two longs, as will appear below. The second note is called the long and is written thus: . And it is named long because it has a certain length greater than the value of any note in plainchant as most commonly sung. The third is called the breve or *tempus* and is written thus: . And it is called a breve because it has the brevity of value most commonly used in plainchant; it is called *tempus* because its value is that of the *tempus* or *mensura*, i.e., the *tempus* or *mensura* most commonly used for the singing of plainchant.[1] The fourth is called semibreve and is written thus: . And it is named semibreve either in the sense of an incomplete breve *(semabrevis)*,[2] or because it is sometimes half of a breve, as stated below. The fifth is called the minim and is written thus: . And it is named minim because, before the invention of the semiminim, it had the minimum[3] value of the five notes then in use, and the inventors of the semiminim and their successors were reluctant to change the names that had been given the notes or note-forms of mensural music by the early writers *(antiquis)*. The sixth and last is called the semiminim, and it is written in two ways, first like a minim except that a flag with no upward hook is appended to the stem, thus: . Semiminims of this sort are sung in duple proportion to minims, e.g., two of these semiminims to one minim. The second way is also like a minim, except that a flag with an upward hook is appended to the stem, thus: . Semiminims of this sort are sung in *sesquialtera* proportion to minims, i.e., three of these semiminims to two minims. And the reason semiminims of the first group have less value than

[1] Cf. Apel, pp. 378-380.

[2] That is, in the sense of "less than a breve," not necessarily its half. The etymology involved here is discussed by Sartori, p. 82. The same explanation applies, of course, to *semaminima* below.

[3] Ms: *minorem*. See the introduction, p. 7.

semiminims of the second group is because semiminims of the second group have the flag with the upward hook. By virtue of that hook, which represents their effort to return to the value of a minim, they acquire some additional length, and therefore they are made somewhat longer than semiminims of the first group. However, there seems to be no reason why semiminims of the second group are more often sung in *sesquialtera* proportion than in *sesquitertia*, or some other, apart from the authority of the early writers, whom it is not for us to contradict. We should, rather, hold them in respect and esteem for opening up to us the possibilities of mensural music and thereby conferring a great benefit upon us. And this sixth note is named semiminim either in the sense of an incomplete minim *(semaminima)* or because it is sometimes half a minim, as I said above.

Now, you must realize that you will find many other notes besides these six; but the fact of the matter is that notes have to be given one of the names of the six notes listed above, and therefore you should take care that any note different from these six be named after that one which it most closely resembles. You must know too that the six notes cited above are the basic note-forms,[4] whereas others different from these are not the basic note-forms, although they bear some resemblance to them and therefore have to be related to one of these six, as I said.

Moreover, it must be noted that each of the first four notes of the six listed above has a twofold function, for each can be perfect as a whole and imperfect as a whole. Any of these is perfect as a whole when it is worth three of the next smaller note value, but imperfect as a whole when it is worth two; for perfection consists in ternary number, imperfection in binary. And in speaking of a

[4] "...in propriis figuris figuratae." In his *Tractatus practicae de musica mensurabili* Prosdocimus explains *notam in sua propria figuratione* as "the natural note," the note "not given a punctus [meaning of course a *punctus perfectionis*], not imperfected by some other note, not left unfilled, not changed in any way, but written simply in its own notation." ("...est notandum quod hic per notam de sui natura intelligo notam in sua propria figuratione, non punctatam, nec ab aliqua nota vero imperfectam, nec evacuatam, nec aliquo modo variatam, sed simpliciter in sui figuratione positam.") See Coussemaker III, 202 B.

note as being the next smaller to another, or not the next smaller, I understand them to be arranged in the order given above. Thus, for instance, when a *maxima* has a value of three longs, it is said to be perfect as a whole since the long is said to be the next smaller note after the *maxima*, because in the order of the six notes as presented above — i.e., *maxima*, long, breve, semibreve, minim, and semiminim — the long comes directly after the *maxima*. By analogy, a long is said to be perfect as a whole when it has a value of three breves, but imperfect as a whole when it has a value of two, because the breve comes directly after the long and not directly after the *maxima*, as is obvious. A breve, then, is perfect as a whole when it has a value of three semibreves, but imperfect as a whole when it has a value of two, because the semibreve comes directly after the breve and not directly after the long and the *maxima*. A semibreve, then, is perfect as a whole when it has a value of three minims, but imperfect as a whole when it has a value of two, because the minim comes directly after the semibreve and not directly after the breve, the long, and the *maxima*.

Moreover, each of the first three notes, that is, the *maxima*, the long, and the breve, functions doubly in yet another respect, for each of these can be perfect or imperfect in regard to a part or parts [of the larger value]. Any of these notes is perfect in one or more parts whenever a part or parts of that which is said in such wise to be perfect is perfect, but imperfect in a part or parts whenever a part or parts of that which is said in such wise to be imperfect is imperfect. To explain: Any shorter note is said to be a part of a longer one. Thus a *maxima* is said to be perfect in a part or parts whenever any one of its longs or breves or semibreves, or more than one of its longs or breves or semibreves, or all of them, are perfect. But it is said to be imperfect in a part or parts whenever any one of its longs or breves or semibreves, or more than one of its longs or breves or semibreves, or all of them, are imperfect. And a long is said to be perfect in a part or parts whenever any one of its breves or semibreves, or more than one of its breves or semibreves, or all of them, are perfect. But it is imperfect in a part or parts whenever any one of its breves or semibreves, or more than one of its breves or semibreves, or all of them, are imperfect. And a breve is said to be perfect in a part or parts whenever any one of its semibreves, or more than one of its semibreves, or all of them, are perfect. But it is said to be imperfect in a part or parts whenever any one of its semibreves, or more than one of its semibreves, or all of them, are imperfect.

The minim and the semiminim, however, are in no wise said to be perfect or imperfect, neither as a whole nor in a part or parts, because in their basic notation they are never divisible into three equal parts. To understand this you must know that those and only those notes are said to assume perfection or imperfection which, in their basic notation, can sometimes be divided into three equal parts; oherwise not. And whenever any note, in its basic notation, is divisible into three equal parts in respect to its whole or in respect to some part of itself, then it can be imperfected by the removal of that third part; and whenever such division is not possible, neither is imperfection possible.

[The mensurations]

Having disposed of these matters, let us proceed to an explanation of measure *(mensura)*, seeing that measurement is necessary in all things. Now, although it is possible to treat of many different kinds of measure, I shall at present address myself only to measure in music, which is the subject of our attention at the moment. I say, then, that according to Italian thinking musical measure has to be defined thus: it is the fixing *(divisio)*[5] of the value of a note, perfect or imperfect, [as] notated in its basic notation, whatever that may be; and this [determination of value] is revealed through a *punctus* or its equivalent

[5] See the remarks in the introduction on the meaning of the terms *divisio* and *dividere*.

as applied within the total context of a piece of music. This measure [mensuration], moreover, is of two sorts, for there is one mensuration called *modus* — although some ignorant Italians say that this mensuration is not found among the Italians; but this is not true, for Marchettus of Padua makes much mention of this very *modus* in his *Pomerium*, and any number of others who wrote earlier on this Italian practice have done the same. In fact, I will even go so far as to say to you that the French got this mensuration from the Italians, for the Italian practice is very much older than the French, so I have found, and this is quite apparent from the way all Europeans notate music for organs, flutes, and other instruments, for in this music they distinguish the *tempora* from one another just like the Italians, as anyone of sound understanding can certainly see. *Tempus*, however, is another degree of mensuration.

Now, the mensuration which is called *modus* is again of two kinds, for there is a certain *modus maximarum* and a certain *modus longarum*. *Modus maximarum* is the mensuration whose perfection and imperfection has to be determined or distinguished by the perfection and imperfection of *maximae*. And this *modus maximarum* is also of two kinds, for there is a *modus maximarum perfectus* and a *modus maximarum imperfectus*. *Modus maximarum perfectus* is the *modus maximarum* which assigns the value of three equal longs to all *maximae*, whereas the *imperfectus* is that which assigns them the value of two. Therefore, that piece is in *modus maximarum perfectus* in which all *maximae* are by nature perfect as a whole and in which, between any two successive *puncti* or the equivalents of those *puncti* marking such a *modus maximarum*, there is enclosed the value of a *maxima* that is perfect as a whole; that piece, however, is said to be in *modus maximarum imperfectus* in which all *maximae* are by nature imperfect as a whole and in which, between any two successive *puncti* or their equivalents marking off such a *modus maximarum*, there is enclosed the value of a *maxima* that is imperfect as a whole. And the notes that are perfect or imperfect *by nature (de sui natura)* I understand to be those notes which have not been imperfected by shorter notes or equivalent rests.

*Modus longarum*, on the other hand, is the mensuration whose perfection and imperfection has to be determined or distinguished by the perfection and imperfection of longs. And this *modus longarum* is also of two kinds, for there is a *modus longarum perfectus* and a *modus longarum imperfectus. Modus longarum perfectus* is the *modus longarum* which assigns to longs the value of three equal breves, whereas the *imperfectus* is that which assigns them the value of two. Therefore, that piece is said to be in *modus longarum perfectus* in which all longs are by nature perfect as a whole and in which, between any two successive *puncti* or their equivalents marking off such a *modus longarum*, there is enclosed the value of a long that is perfect as a whole; but that piece is said to be in *modus longarum imperfectus* in which, between any two successive *puncti* or their equivalents marking off such a *modus longarum*, there is enclosed the value of a long that is imperfect as a whole.

The other mensuration, the one called *tempus*, is the mensuration whose perfection and imperfection has to be determined or distinguished by the perfection and imperfection of breves. And this again is of two kinds, for there is a *tempus perfectum* and a *tempus imperfectum. Tempus perfectum* is the *tempus* which assigns to breves the value of three equal semibreves; and this is of three sorts: *tempus senarium*, *tempus novenarium*, and *tempus duodenarium*.

*Tempus senarium perfectum* is the *tempus perfectum* which assigns to breves the value of three equal semibreves or six minims. Hence that piece is *senaria perfecta* in which all breves are by nature perfect as a whole, with a value of six minims, and in which, between any two successive *puncti* or their equivalents marking off such a *tempus*, there is enclosed the value of three equal semibreves of a value of six minims. And it is called *tempus senarium* because any breve — a breve being also called a *tempus*, as I have said — any breve found in this mensuration has by nature the value of six minims.

*Tempus novenarium*, however, is the *tempus perfectum* which assigns to breves the value of three equal semibreves worth nine minims. Hence that piece is said to be *novenaria* in which all breves are by nature perfect as a whole, having the value of nine minims, and in which, between any two successive *puncti* or their equivalents marking off such a *tempus*, there is enclosed the value of three equal semibreves worth nine minims. And it is called *tempus novenarium* because any breve found in this mensuration has by nature the value of nine minims.

*Tempus duodenarium*, however, is the *tempus perfectum* which assigns to breves the value of three equal semibreves worth twelve minims. Hence that piece is *duodenaria* in which all breves are by nature perfect as a whole, having a value of twelve minims, and in which, between any two successive *puncti* or their equivalents marking off such a *tempus*, there is enclosed the value of three equal semibreves worth twelve minims. And it is called *tempus duodenarium* because any breve found in this mensuration has by its nature the value of twelve minims.

*Tempus imperfectum*, on the other hand, is the *tempus* whose breves are worth only two equal semibreves. It is of three kinds: *tempus quaternarium*, *tempus senarium*, and *tempus octenarium*.

*Tempus quaternarium* is the *tempus imperfectum* whose breves are worth two equal semibreves having the value of four minims. Hence that piece is *quaternaria* in which all breves are imperfect as a whole and in their parts, with a value of four minims, and in which, between any two successive *puncti* or their equivalents marking off such a *tempus*, there is enclosed the value of two equal semibreves worth four minims. And it is called *tempus quaternarium* because any breve found in this mensuration has a value of four minims.

*Tempus senarium imperfectum*, however, is the *tempus imperfectum* whose breves have the value of two equal semibreves worth six minims. Hence that piece is *senaria imperfecta* in which all its breves are imperfect as a whole, though having the value of six minims, and in which, between any two successive *puncti* or their equivalents marking off such a *tempus*, there is enclosed the value of two equal semibreves worth six minims. And it is called *tempus senarium* because any breve found in this mensuration has by its nature the value of six minims. And thus you know how it is that there are two kinds of *tempus senarium*, namely perfect and imperfect, and how one may be distinguished from the other.

*Tempus octenarium*, however, is the *tempus imperfectum* which provides breves having the value of two equal semibreves worth eight minims. Hence that piece is *octenaria* in which all breves are imperfect as a whole and in their parts too, and they have the value of eight minims. Moreover, between any two successive *puncti* or their equivalents marking off such a *tempus*, there is enclosed the value of two equal semibreves worth eight minims. And *tempus octenarium* bears this name because any breve found in this mensuration has the value of eight minims.

You know now, then, how many mensurations are in use among the Italians and how they may be recognized and distinguished from one another.

But the reason we do not speak of *novenarium perfectum* and *duodenarium perfectum* as we speak of *senarium perfectum*, aside from the fact that all such *tempora* are perfect, and likewise the reason we do not speak of *quaternarium imperfectum* and of *octenarium imperfectum* as we speak of *senarium imperfectum*, aside from the fact that all such *tempora* are imperfect, is that, since there are two kinds of *senarium*, perfect and imperfect, as we have seen, it is in consequence necessary to apply these terms, perfect and imperfect, to them in order to distinguish the one *senarium* from the other; but as this duality *(multiplicitas)*, and the resulting need for the differentiating terms, is not found among the other mensurations just mentioned, we do not in consequence apply these terms, perfect and imperfect, to them. We could apply them if we liked, but it would be to no purpose.

Now, it must be noted that there are those who set up a *tempus ternarium* as another mensuration in addition to the others. They say that *tempus ternarium* is that which assigns to the breve a value of three minims. They say, then, that that piece is *ternaria* in which all breves have by nature a value of three minims and in which, between any two successive *puncti* or their equivalents marking off such a *tempus*, there is enclosed the value of three minims. And they say it is called *tempus ternarium* because any breve found in such a measure has by nature the value of three minims. But all this seems quite absurd to me for two reasons. The first is that no note is ever seen to acquire the value of a *nota recta* [unaltered note] of lesser value, although, as we know, a note can readily acquire the value of a note of greater value, i.e., through alteration. The second reason is that we would have a *tempus* that is neither perfect nor imperfect. *Tempus ternarium* would not be perfect for, if it were, the breve would naturally have the value of three semibreves, which it does not have in this case; nor would it be imperfect for, if it were, the breve would have the value of two semibreves, which it also does not have in this case. And were you to say that *tempus ternarium* is perfect because the breve has by its nature the value of three minims, I would say in reply that a perfection of this value does not pertain to perfection of the *tempus*, or breve, but to perfection of the semibreve, as explained above. Therefore let us dismiss this mensuration as superfluous and contrary to reason.

Now, these mensurations were invented so that, whenever we are confronted with a piece of music, we may know at once the value of any note of variable value found in that piece. And [so] to each of the first three notes listed above, i.e., the *maxima*, the long, and the breve, is assigned one of these mensurations. To the *maxima* is assigned the *modus maximarum* because [this mensuration] has to be known by the perfection and imperfection of *maximae*. To the long is assigned the *modus longarum* because [this mensuration] has to be known by the perfection and imperfection of longs. And to the breve is assigned the *tempus* because [this mensuration] has to be known by the perfection and imperfection of breves.

And no mensuration is assigned to any of the other notes, i.e., semibreve, minim, and semiminim, because no note can have a mensuration assigned to it unless it is one that is variable in value, as the *maxima*, the long, the breve, and the semibreve are, because the value of these notes is known by means of these very mensurations, as we have said; and therefore the minim and the semiminim have no mensuration assigned to them since neither is ever variable in value, at least when notated in their normal manner.

Furthermore, the reason why the semibreve has no mensuration assigned to it, even though it too is variable in value, is that one of the mensurations already named, i.e., *tempus*, enables us to know the value of any semibreve found in a piece of music readily enough without the setting up of another mensuration. Therefore, no mensuration is assigned to the semibreve because to invent one for it would be to create a needless profusion, which is considered the greatest fault in any art because art should follow Nature as closely as possible, as Aristotle says in book ii of the Physics;[6] and Nature no more abounds in the superfluous than she is deficient in the essential, as Aristotle again says, this time in book iii of the *De anima*.[7] Therefore, the French are quite wrong in establishing four mensurations — that is, the two *modi*, *tempus*, and *prolatio* — when only three, the two *modi* plus *tempus*, are enough, as we have seen; in so doing they create a needless profusion, which is the greatest fault in art, as I have said. In this, then, they should not find approval.

The reason why the mensuration called *tempus* is assigned to the breve rather than to the semibreve, even though the value of

[6] Apparently a reference to the famous dictum that art is an imitation of nature. See *Physica* 11.2 (194 a).

[7] There are two remarks in book iii that could be construed as sources for this statement: "If nature, then,neither does anything without a purpose nor omits anything that is necessary..." ('Ει οὖν ἡ φύσις μήτε ποιεῖ μάτην μηθὲν μήτε ἀπολείπει τι τῶν ἀναγκαίων...) And: "An animal necessarily has sensation if nature does nothing without a purpose. For everything in nature is there to an end, or exists as a concomitant of things that are there to an end." (τὸ δὲ ςῷον ἀναγκαῖον αἴσθησιν ἔχειν, εἰ μηθὲν μάτην ποιεῖ ἡ φύσις. Ένεκά του γὰρ ἅπαντα ὑπάρχει τὰ φύσει, ἢ συμπτώματα ἔσται τῶν ἕνεκά του.) *De anima* iii.9 (432 b) and iii.12 (434 a).

both has to be discovered by means of the same mensuration, is this, that since it is right and proper for the greater to take precedence over the lesser, this mensuration is [therefore] assigned to the note of greater value, i.e., the breve, and not to the note of lesser value [i.e., the semibreve]. It is also because[8] this mensuration, otherwise called "*tempus*," has the name "breve," as I said before. Another reason is that the value of the breve is known directly by means of this mensuration, whereas that of the semibreve is known indirectly or at second hand, as anyone can see. Thus, if I know the *tempus* to be perfect, I know that the breve has by its nature the value of three equal semibreves. And if I know it to be *senarium*, I know in consequence that each of its semibreves is imperfect, and likewise if I know it to be *duodenarium*; but if I know it to be *novenarium*, I know thereby that each of its semibreves is perfect by nature. On the other hand, if I know the *tempus* to be imperfect, I know that the breve has a value of two equal semibreves. And if I know it to *quaternarium*, then I know that each of its semibreves is imperfect, and likewise if I know it to be *octenarium*; but if I know it to be *senarium*, I know in consequence that each of its semibreves is perfect by nature.

Also it must be noted that in the modal mensurations the Italians enclose every *modus* or every *modus* value, whether perfect or imperfect — it matters not which — within two *puncti* or their equivalents; and in the temporal mensurations they likewise enclose every *tempus* or *tempus* value, whether perfect or imperfect — it matters not which — within two *puncti* or their equivalents. And they do this for greater clarity so that, when we are confronted with a piece of music, we may know at once what its mensuration is, whether it has perfection or imperfection and what perfection or imperfection it has, and which note is perfect, which imperfect, which has lesser

[8] The manuscript reading, *praeterea quia*, is followed here rather than Sartori's *propter quod* (see the introduction, p. 5). With the latter the sentence would translate, "On this account [i.e., because the mensuration in question is assigned to the breve] this mensuration, otherwise called *tempus*, assumes the name breve..." This, to be sure, is more logical than the original, which seems to say that the mensuration in question is assigned to the breve because "breve" is one of the names for it!

value and which greater; and in addition, how we may count the *modi* and the *tempora* quickly and easily and distinguish them from one another.

I have used the phrase "their equivalents" because any note and its rest in the measure assigned to it, and also any longer note and its rest, as well as any ligature in its *divisio*,[9] take the place of a *punctus*, except where we may want to separate a shorter note from a longer by means of a *punctus*. Suppose, for instance, that in *tempus perfectum* there is a single breve placed first followed by a single semibreve, then another breve, and that breve by several other notes all shorter than the breve itself; and suppose we want to separate the first semibreve from the first breve. Then we have to put a *punctus* just before that first semibreve because otherwise the first breve would be imperfected by the semibreve. And you could not in this case change the second breve to a semibreve, nor could you alter it, as many ignorant Italian musicians do every day, because there is no necessity for alteration here and alteration should never be made except where it is necessary, as will be made abundantly clear in what follows. In this case, then, the first breve does not take the place of a *punctus* since a *punctus* must of necessity be placed between it and the semibreve directly following, but it is true that the aforementioned things do take the place of a *punctus* for the most part.

And the reason why these three things take the place of a *punctus* for the most part is this: first, with regard to the note or rest to which a mensuration is assigned: Any note or its rest within its own measure has by nature the perfection or imperfection which it is supposed to have, this being what the mensuration tells us, as I have explained, and thus there is no need for a *punctus* to show us this; therefore [such a note or rest] takes the place of a *punctus*, as I just said. But with regard to the longer notes and their rests, the reason is that they contain the shorter notes and their rests: If the shorter

[9] This is the one instance in the treatise in which *divisio* is used as equivalent to *mensura*, "mensuration" or "measure." See the observations in the introduction on the use of these terms.

notes and their rests within their own measures indicate the completion of the perfection or imperfection of the measure without a *punctus* and so take the place of a *punctus* for the most part, as I have just explained, then we have to say likewise that the longer notes and their rests indicate the completion of the perfection or imperfection of a measure of the shorter note without a *punctus* and thus also take the place of a *punctus*. And it is obvious that a ligature may also take the place of a *punctus* and especially when it is a ligature of notes shorter than the note or rest to which the mensuration is assigned — because when notes greater than or equal to this value are ligated, there is no question, as I just explained — since the ligating of these shorter values is an indication that they have been ligated simply in order to complete the perfection or imperfection of the note or rest to which the mensuration is assigned, which is a logical reason for their being ligated, and thus they too take the place of a *punctus*, as I said above.

Nor should the Italian complain of so many *puncti*, for they are all required to clarify practice and therefore they are not used unnecessarily.

Now, from the foregoing it is obvious that the Italian practice is finer and more estimable than the French because, of any two practices tending to the same end, that one which is the clearer will be the finer and the more estimable; and these two practices, the French and the Italian, both tend to the same end, the end of both being the performance of mensural music, and the Italian is the clearer, as anybody can see who is expert in both, and therefore it is the finer and the more estimable.

Moreover, for greater clarity in this practice the Italians use only one kind of *punctus*, the *punctus divisionis*. The reason for this is that if they were to use two kinds — that is, the *punctus perfectionis* and the *punctus divisionis* — as the French do, they would thereby render their practice less clear, as the French practice is rendered by the two kinds of *puncti*, because there would very often be an uncertainty at first glance as to the effect of these *puncti*, that is, whether they should serve to perfect or to divide, as frequently happens with the French. Still another reason can be given: this *punctus [perfectionis]* would be used to perfect a note either in the perfection of its mensuration or in its imperfection; [but it would] not [perfect a note] in the perfection of its mensuration because there the note is just as perfect without a *punctus* as with one, being perfect by nature, and so its use would be superfluous. Nor [should it be used] in the imperfection of a note's mensuration because there it would change it from what it is by nature; and thus, for instance, a breve which ought to be *quaternaria* would become *senaria*; and one that ought to be *senaria*, *novenaria*; and one that ought to be *novenaria*, *duodenaria* — which is quite illogical because in any *simplex* piece, i.e., a piece in only one mensuration, all the notes to which that mensuration is assigned should have one and the same value. It follows, then, that there should be only one *punctus*, the *punctus divisionis*, because there is no requirement that compels us to use the other *punctus*, the *punctus perfectionis*, since we can do quite well without it, as we have seen. And the French are in error here too because in using the *punctus perfectionis*, which is not necessary in practice, they create a needless profusion, and this, as I have said, is the greatest fault in an art. And although this is true, there are nevertheless capricious and irrational musicians even among the Italians who sometimes use a *punctus* to perfect notes in a piece that is notated according to Italian practice, calling this *punctus* the *punctus perfectionis*. In so doing they create a profusion of *puncti*, both unnecessarily, as we have seen, and improperly. Therefore, no attention should be paid to these people for the reasons adduced above.

And as I have just made mention of music in *simplex* mensuration, it must be noted that in this practice there are two types of mensural music, namely the simple and the composite or mixed. A piece in simple mensuration is one which is in, or one whose sections are in, a single mensuration, i.e., one of those listed above. The composite or mixed, on the other hand, is one which is not in, or whose sections are not in, a single mensuration but in more than one of those listed above. And all of this is indicated by *puncti* marking the measures.

Now, although these *puncti* are sufficient to indicate the mensurations to us, it is customary nevertheless to provide other, extrinsic signs which distinguish the mensurations more clearly. Some of these signs are more general, others more special. There are many general signs. For instance, to indicate perfection a bar is sometimes drawn through the staff with three dots after it, denoting the number 3, in which perfection consists, thus: |⋮ And for imperfection, the same with two dots denoting the number 2, in which imperfection consists, thus: |:

But sometimes for perfection they use the letter T denoting *ternary* number, in which again perfection consists; and for imperfection, the letter B denoting *binary* number, in which again imperfection consists. Also, for perfection the letter P denoting *perfection* is sometimes used, and for imperfection the letter I denoting *imperfection.* The special signs are as follows: for the perfect *modus maximarum* a double N is used with the letter P, denoting *modus maximarum perfectus,* thus: NNP; and for the imperfect, a double N with the letter I denoting *modus maximarum imperfectus,* thus: NNI. For the perfect *modus longarum* the three letters N, L and P are used, denoting *modus longarum perfectus,* thus: NLP; and for the imperfect *modus longarum* these three letters are used, N, L, and I, denoting *modus longarum imperfectus,* thus: NLI. For any perfect *tempus* two letters are used, T and P, denoting *tempus perfectum,* thus: TP; and two letters are also used for any imperfect *tempus,* T and I, denoting *tempus imperfectum,* thus: TI. But for a *tempus* it is customary to use still more special signs. Thus, for *tempus quaternarium* the letter Q is used, denoting *quaternaria* mensuration; and for the perfect *tempus senarium* these two letters are used, SP, denoting tempus *senarium perfectum*; and for the imperfect *tempus senarium* these two letters are used, SI, denoting tempus *senarium imperfectum*; and for *tempus octenarium* the letter O is used denoting tempus *octenarium*; and for *novenarium* the letter n is used denoting tempus *novenarium*; and for tempus *duodenarium* the letter D is used denoting tempus *duodenarium*.

All these are the signs which enable us to distinguish one mensuration from another without using different colors and without leaving notes unfilled, both of which are characteristic of French practice, and unnecessary, since the above signs are plainly sufficient. It appears, then, that the French practice is superfluous, as is quite evident to anybody who cares to look into the matter closely.

Nor should anyone say that the Italian practice creates an unnecessary profusion in setting up an *octenaria* mensuration, which might appear to be double *quaternaria*, and a *duodenaria* mensuration, which might appear to be triple *quaternaria*, when the said multiples of *quaternaria* would appear to suffice for the purpose. For if we consider the matter carefully, [we will see that] these two mensurations, *duodenaria* and *octenaria*, have not been set up unnecessarily. For this purpose you must know that between the minim and that semiminim which is sung in duple proportion to the minim there are two other values, both rationally calculable and delightful to sing. One is sesquialteral to the minim, and it is for this value that the semiminims with the upward hook to the flag, mentioned above, were invented. The other is sesquitertial to the minim, and for this value the two mensurations just mentioned were invented, i.e., *octenaria* and *duodenaria*. If we calculate these mensurations carefully and [then] sing them somewhat fast *(aliquantulum stricte)*, we will find the *octenaria* mensuration reduced to the *senaria*, and *duodenaria* to *novenaria*. The two larger measures, you see, are in *proportio sesquitertia* [respectively] to the two smaller. Therefore, these mensurations have not been set up unnecessarily, because we could not have this sesquitertial proportion without them. But of course they would have been set up unnecessarily if they were sung as notated (*sub suo proprio esse*) instead of faster, that is, *octenaria* as double *quaternaria*, and *duodenaria* as triple *quaternaria*, as they are sometimes sung by ignorant Italian musicians. These men claim that *tempus octenarium* and *tempus duodenarium* do not always have to be sung in *proportio sesquitertia* to *senarium* and *novenarium,* but that sometimes *octenarium* should be sung as double *quaternarium* and *duodenarium* as triple *quaternarium.* But no heed should be paid to such people, because what they say is improper and untrue, for the reasons already adduced. And if someone should yet insist, in rebuttal to this, that the mensurations in question, that is *octenaria* and *duodenaria,* have still been set up unnecessarily since the *quaternaria* mensuration, if sung faster, would suffice to produce the *proportio sesquitertia,* as any intelligent person can see, it would certainly have to be conceded in reply that the *quaternaria* mensuration, if sung faster, would be sufficient for the *proportio sesquitertia.* But I say that you must not on that account maintain that the two mensurations in question have been set up unnecessarily and that the *quaternaria* mensuration ought to be used for *proportio sesquitertia*; because, if these two mensurations were not provided and the *quaternaria* mensuration were sometimes to stand for *proportio sesquitertia,* then every time we were confronted with a piece of music in *quaternaria* mensuration, we would be in doubt whether the notes should be sung according to their own values, that is, full length, or whether they should be sung shorter, that is, in *proportio sesquitertia.* It was in order to avoid this ambiguity that the two mensurations in question, *octenaria* and *duodenaria,* were invented. In this way, we know that *tempus quaternarium* is always to be sung as *quaternaria,* and *octenaria* and *duodenaria* always in *proportio sesquitertia* to *senaria* and *novenaria.* And now you know why these mensurations have not been set up unnecessarily, which is what we wanted to make clear.

Also, if someone should ask why a mensuration has not been devised which could be sung in *proportio sesquitertia* to *tempus quaternarium* as [*octenaria and duodenaria are*] to *senaria* and *novenaria,* the answer would have to be that this is simply because there is no number that can be found in *proportio sesquitertia* to 4 in the way that [numbers can obviously be found in that proportion] to 6 and 9. For this to happen, one would have to be able to divide 4 into three equal parts, and this is not possible, at least insofar as integers are concerned, which is what I am talking about here; and therefore, etc.

[Alteration]

Now, a knowledge of alteration is necessary for an understanding of what follows, and therefore we must discuss alteration itself somewhat so that what comes later can be understood more easily.

This, then, is the definition of alteration: alteration is the doubling of the normal value of the note to be altered. From this it follows that to alter is nothing more than to give the note to be altered twice its normal value. Thus, an altered long has the value of two longs; an altered breve has the value of two breves; and so on. Now, this musical alteration is analogous to natural alteration, for just as in natural alteration the thing altered is changed from one quality to another — for example, from white to red, or from cold to hot, etc. — so in this musical alteration the note altered is changed from one value to another, namely from its normal value to twice that. However, not every change in value is to be called an alteration but only the change to double value, as I have said.

The first thing you must know about this musical alteration is that it was devised in order to make possible the completion of the perfection or imperfection [i.e., the perfect or imperfect measure] of any note subject to perfection or imperfection when that value could not otherwise be completed. From this it follows, first, that alteration should never be made except where necessary and, secondly, that the *maxima* and the semiminim can in no wise be altered because it is apparent that neither of these notes has to be altered in order to complete the value of any perfect or imperfect note. Also, alteration of the semiminim is unnecessary for still another reason, namely that, unlike the other alterable notes, it can be changed to [i.e., written as] the next longer note, as will appear below. And so you know why there are only four alterable notes: the long, the breve, the semibreve, and the minim.

The long is altered only to complete the value of a perfect *maxima*, and it has to be altered only in *modus maximarum perfectus*. The breve is altered only to complete the value of a perfect long, and only in *modus longarum perfectus* does it have to be altered. The semibreve, however, is altered to complete the value of either a perfect or an imperfect breve, and thus it can be altered in every *tempus* except *quaternarium* and *senarium imperfectum*. But the minim is altered only to complete the value of a perfect semibreve, and thus it cannot be altered except in *senarium imperfectum* and in *novenarium*,

Moreover, you should know that the semibreve is altered in two ways, with a sign and without a sign. The semibreve is altered without a sign when it is altered without changing its regular shape; but it is altered with a sign when it is altered by means of a stem drawn downward. And you should realize that this downward stem added to the regular form of the semibreve is a quite logical sign of alteration because, just as a semibreve acquires the value of the next shorter note, namely of the minim, by means of an upward stem added to its regular form, so it follows that by means of a downward stem added to its regular form, it must acquire the value of the next longer note, namely of a breve, at least of an imperfect breve, which is the value it acquires by alteration.

And since we have just now spoken of stems, you should know that, if a stem descending at an angle is added to a semibreve, that stem increases the value of such a semibreve by a half. And the reason is this: if the value of a semibreve is increased by the addition to it of a stem drawn straight down, as we have seen, then it follows that its value must also be increased by a stem drawn down at an angle, since this stem also descends; but because it descends at an angle and not straight, it is logical that it does not increase the value as much as the stem which descends vertically; rather, since it occupies a mean position, so to speak, it should therefore increase the value of a semibreve by a half, because obviously the value in question when it is increased by half is the mean, so to speak, between the regular or unaltered value of the note and the value to which it is increased by that stem which is drawn straight down. From this, then, you can see how incorrect many people's notation is in this practice when, for example, they append a stem ascending at an angle to a semibreve in order to give it the value of three minims, thereby diminishing it where they think to augment it, for, as we have seen, an ascending stem has the effect of reducing value.

[Rules for note values]

And now that we have covered these useful preliminaries, we must consider in detail the values of notes varying in value as they are found in pieces of music, a subject you will be able to understand easily and sufficiently with the help of the following rules.

The first rule, then, is this: a *maxima* before a *maxima* or its rest in *modus maximarum perfectus*, and a long before a long or its rest in *modus longarum perfectus*, and a breve before a breve [or its rest] in *tempus perfectum*, and a semibreve before a semibreve or its rest in *senarium imperfectum* or *novenarium* is always perfect as a whole. And the reason for this is that, if it were otherwise and we wanted to complete a syncopation with *(per sincopam reducere)* a single long after more than one *maxima* in a piece in *modus maximarum perfectus*, or with a single breve after more than one long in a piece in *modus longarum perfectus*, or with a single semibreve after more than one breve in a piece in *tempus perfectum*, or with a single minim after more than one semibreve in a piece in *senarium imperfectum* or *novenarium*, we could not do so without putting signs of some sort at the place where we wanted to make such syncopations. But since, by keeping our rule, we can do this quite well without such signs, it follows that this rule has been sensibly made, because there is no purpose in doing with many things what can be done with fewer, as Aristotle says in books i and viii of the *Physics*.[10]

Now I said "as a whole" because this is not necessary in respect to a part or parts, e.g., in the case of *maximae* in a piece in *modus maximarum perfectus* and *modus longarum imperfectus*, and in the case of longs in *modus longarum perfectus* and *tempus imperfectum*, and in the case of breves in *tempus senarium perfectum*.

It follows from this rule, first, that if any note subject to imperfection is to be imperfected as a whole by a part preceding *(a parte ante)*, it should be followed directly by a value longer or shorter than itself, either as a note or a rest. Secondly, it follows that a value preceding the same value *(similis ante similem)*, either as a note or a rest, can in no wise be imperfected as a whole.

Here is an example of the rule:

The second rule is as follows: if in *modus maximarum perfectus* a single long is found between two *maximae*, or between a *maxima* and its rest, or a *maxima* and a *punctus*, that long imperfects the first *maxima* as a whole unless prevented by a *punctus* or in some other way; thus:[11]

[10] Cf. *Physica* 1.6 (189 a): "...also because a finite number suffices. And a finite number, as Empedocles [provides], is better than an infinite number; for he [Empedocles] bethinks him to render [with his finite number of principles] all that Anaxagoras does with an infinite number." (καὶ ὅτι ἐνδέχεται ἐκ πεπερασμένων. βέλτιον δ'εκ πεπερασμένων, ὥσπερ Ἐμπεδοκλῆς, ἢ ἐξ ἀπείρων· πάντα γὰρ ἀποδιδόναι οἴεται ὅσα περ Ἀναξαγόρας ἐκ τῶν ἀπείρων.) And viii.6 (259 a): "One should always expect unity rather than diversity, and finitude rather than infinitude; for, by preference, we should always assume a finite number of things, since in the things that constitute nature the finite and the better should be present, by preference, if possible." (ἓν δὲ μᾶλλον ἢ πολλὰ καὶ πεπερασμένα ἢ ἀπείρα δεῖ νομίςειν. τῶν αὐτῶν γὰρ συμβαινόντων ἀεὶ τὰ πεπερασμένα μᾶλλον ληπτέον· ἐν γὰρ τοῖς φύσει δεῖ τὸ πεπερασμένον καὶ τὸ βέλτιον, ἂν ἐνδέχηται, ὑπαρχειν μᾶλλον.)

[11] The next nine examples are transcribed on the basis of perfection in all mensurations, with B (♩.) = 9 Mi, making the tempus N. Also, for simplicity, the barring is based upon the equivalence of one measure to the perfection of the longest value involved except in the last instance where it is equivalent to 1 B.

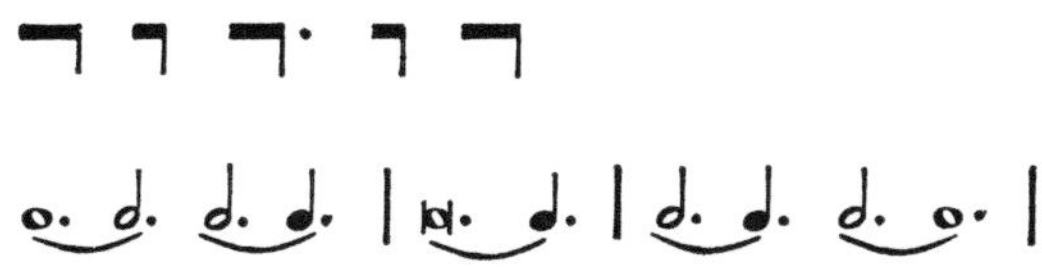

And the reason for this is that any note imperfected by a part of its value, where that part is the note next shorter than itself, its imperfected as a whole.

But if in *modus longarum perfectus* a single breve is found between two *maximae*, or a *maxima* and its rest, or a *maxima* and a *punctus*, that breve imperfects the first *maxima* by one of its parts, namely a long, unless prevented by a *punctus* or in some other way; thus:

And if in *tempus perfectum* a single semibreve is found between two *maximae*, or a *maxima* and its rest, or a *maxima* and a *punctus*, that semibreve imperfects the first *maxima* by one of its parts, namely a breve, unless prevented by a *punctus* or in some other way; thus:

And if in *senaria imperfecta* or *novenaria* a minim is found between two *maximae*, or a *maxima* and its rest, or a *maxima* and a *punctus*, that minim imperfects the first *maxima* by one of its parts, namely a semibreve, unless prevented by a *punctus* or in some other way; thus:

It is the same with longs:

If in *modus longarum perfectus* a single breve is found between two longs, or a long and its rest, or a long and a *punctus*, that breve imperfects the first long as a whole, unless prevented by a *punctus* or in some other way; thus:

But if in *tempus perfectum* a single semibreve is found between two longs, or a long and its rest, or a long and a *punctus*, that semibreve imperfects the first long by one of its parts, namely a breve, unless prevented by a *punctus* or in some other way; thus:

And if in *senaria imperfecta* or *novenaria* a single minim is found between two longs, or a long and its rest, or a long and a *punctus*, that minim imperfects the first long by one of its parts, namely a semibreve, unless prevented by a *punctus* or in some other way; thus:

It is the same with breves:

If in *tempus perfectum* a single semibreve is found between two breves, or a breve and its rest, or a breve and a *punctus*, that semibreve imperfects the first breve as a whole unless prevented by a *punctus* or in some other way; thus:

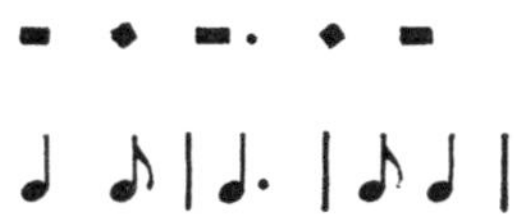

But if in *senaria imperfecta* or *novenaria* a single minim is found between two breves, or a breve and its rest, or a breve and a *punctus*, that minim imperfects the first breve by one of its parts, namely a semibreve, unless prevented by a *punctus* or in some other way; thus:

It is the same with semibreves:

If in *senaria perfecta* a single minim or four minims; and if in *novenaria* a single minim, or four or seven minims, are found between two semibreves, or a semibreve and its rest, or a semibreve and a *punctus*; that minim, or the first minim if there is more than one, imperfects the first semibreve as a whole unless prevented by a *punctus* or in some other way; thus:

And the reason for this rule is to have shorter notes follow longer ones in any of the latter's perfections, as anyone can find out for himself with a little experience. And you should know that what has been said about imperfecting notes by other notes holds good whether the latter values are notes or rests.

The third rule is this: if in *modus maximarum perfectus* two longs, or the value thereof in notes or rests, provided the last is a long, are found between two *maximae* or their rests, or between a *punctus* or nothing and a *maxima* or its rest; and likewise, if in *modus longarum perfectus* two breves, or the value thereof in notes or rests, provided the last is a breve, are found between two longs or their rests, or between a *punctus* or nothing and a long or its rest; and likewise, if in *tempus perfectum* two semibreves, or the value thereof in notes or rests, provided the last is a semibreve, are found between two breves or their rests, or between a *punctus* or nothing and a semibreve or its rest; and likewise, if in *senaria imperfecta* two minims, or the value thereof in notes or rests, provided the last is a minim, are found between two semibreves or their rests, or between a *punctus* or nothing and a semibreve or its rest; then the second long or breve or semibreve or minim is invariably altered in order to complete the perfection of the next longer note, unless there is a *punctus* to prevent it, because such perfection cannot be completed otherwise than by alteration; thus:

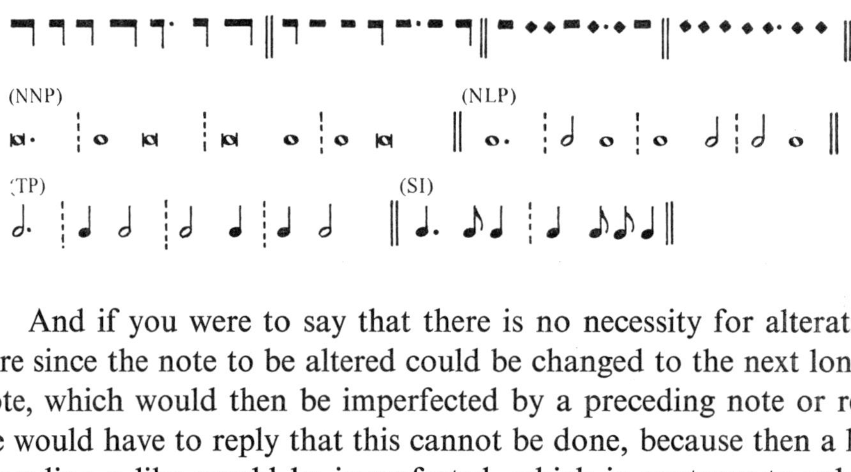


And if you were to say that there is no necessity for alteration here since the note to be altered could be changed to the next longer note, which would then be imperfected by a preceding note or rest, we would have to reply that this cannot be done, because then a like preceding a like would be imperfected, which is contrary to rule 1. This rule also tells you how alteration can be avoided by placing a *punctus* just before an alterable note. But the reason why the last of the two notes is altered rather than the first is for the sake of having an end complete the thing of which it is the end, because the end of anything is its completion, and therefore the last is altered and not the first,[12] unless prevented by a stem [added to the first], as will be explained below in [the rules] concerning *octenaria* and *duodenaria* mensurations. From what has been said, then, it is quite apparent how present-day musicians are at fault when in *tempus perfectum* they alter a semibreve worth one-third of a breve preceding another like itself, or preceding a note shorter than itself, or preceding a longer note which does not directly follow it, when there is no necessity for alteration in such instances since the note that they alter can be changed to the next longer note without any inconvenience, and then a note will be imperfected by a preceding part or a following part, depending upon whether the imperfecting note is placed before or after that which is imperfected.[13]

The fourth rule is this: if before or after any one of the four perfectable and imperfectable notes there are found several shorter values, but not including the next shorter, by which the former can there be imperfected as a whole or by a part or parts, then the note is imperfected as a whole by the sum of those notes if they can constitute a part of it one degree removed from its own value *(partem sibi propinquam)* sufficient to imperfect it in whole, and if they all belong to the same part of the note, since otherwise it would not be imperfected as a whole but only in one or more parts. And all this is understood to hold good unless prevented by a *punctus*. [The reason for] this rule is self-evident because it is plain that [combinations of such values] could not conveniently be arranged otherwise.

The fifth rule is this: when any of the six notes listed above, except the *maxima*, remains isolated after the calculation of some

[12] Prosdocimus enters into this a little more fully in the first redaction of the treatise: "...since the last of the aforesaid notes in the aforesaid perfections, [as] enclosed between two *puncti* or their equivalents marking such perfections, are the end of those perfections, they should therefore complete [fill out] those perfections, which cannot be done otherwise than by alteration, and therefore they must be altered, as our rule says." ("...et cum ultimae supradictarum figurarum in perfectionibus supradictis, clausarum inter duo puncta vel sibi conformia tales perfectiones dividentia, sint finis talium perfectionum, ideo ipsae complere debent tales perfectiones, quod aliter fieri non potest quam per alterationem, et ideo alterari debent ut dicit regula nostra.") See Coussemaker III, 237 A.

[13] Cf. Apel, p. 113.

perfection, it must be assigned to the first place it can take. If there is a note immediately preceding or immediately following, that place will be clear enough; if not, it should be enclosed between two *puncti* to show that it must be assigned to another position. And the same applies if there should be more than one note remaining isolated after the calculation of some perfection.

The sixth rule is this: if in *tempus octenarium*, between two *puncti* or their equivalents marking off such a measure, there are found four semibreves, or three semibreves with two minims, or two semibreves with four minims, or one semibreve with six minims, all these semibreves will have the same value. This is obvious because each of them has a value of two minims, which is the least value to which a semibreve can be reduced, and therefore all of them together constitute eight minims, which make one *tempus octenarium*, as we have seen; thus:

The seventh rule is this: if in *tempus octenarium*, between two *puncti* or their equivalents marking off such a measure, there are found three semibreves regularly notated, or the value thereof in notes or rests, provided any semibreves are there, then in order to complete the measure the last of these semibreves must be altered, [and the last is altered] because it is the concluding note. The reason for this rule was touched upon above in rule 3. You should know too that the alteration of this last note can be prevented by the addition of a [downward] stem to any one of the preceding semibreves, the addition of such a stem being also an indication of alteration, as mentioned above. You should also know that only one semibreve can be altered in *tempus octenarium*, no more, whether such alteration is made with a stem or without a stem. The reason for this is that this is sufficient to complete this *tempus*. An example of the rule is this:

The eighth rule is this: if in *tempus octenarium*, between two *puncti* or their equivalents marking off such a measure, four minims follow one semibreve, or if a semibreve is placed within a group of four minims, then that semibreve has to be altered. The reason for this is that the measure could not otherwise be completed. An example of the rule is this:

The ninth rule is this: semibreves in *octenaria* are never changed by alteration except to the value of four minims. This rule is clear from the preceding rules.

The tenth rule is this: if in *tempus duodenarium*, between two *puncti* or their equivalents marking off such a measure, there are found four semibreves regularly notated, or their value in notes or rests, then the last two are altered, provided they are represented by semibreves. The reason for this rule was touched upon above in rule 3. However, you should know that the preceding semibreves can also be altered, though not without changing the note-forms, hence, by adding descending tails. You should also know that in *tempus duodenarium* only two semibreves can be altered and no more, whether such alteration is made with stems or without stems. The reason is that this is sufficient to complete the measure. An example of the rule is this:

The eleventh rule is this: if in *tempus duodenarium*, between two *puncti* or their equivalents marking off such a measure, there are found four semibreves, or the value thereof, provided the last is a semibreve, and if only one of the first two of these semibreves has the downward stem, which causes it to be altered, then the last of them must also be altered, even though it has its normal note-form, since the measure could not otherwise be completed. Again, the reason for the alteration of this last semibreve is mentioned above in rule 3. An example of the rule is this:

The twelfth rule is this: if in *tempus duodenarium*, between two *puncti* or their equivalents marking off such a measure, there are found five regularly notated semibreves, or their value, then the last of them, provided it is a semibreve, must be altered in order to complete the measure; and any one of the preceding semibreves can also be altered [i.e., instead of the last] if it has a descending tail. This is clear from what has preceded. An example of the rule is this:

The thirteenth rule is this: if in *tempus duodenarium*, between two *puncti* or their equivalents marking off such a measure, there are found six semibreves, or five with two minims, or four with four minims, or three with six minims, or two with eight minims, or one with ten minims, then all the semibreves are of equal value, namely the value of two minims. An example of the rule is this:

The fourteenth rule is this: if in *tempus duodenarium*, between two *puncti* or their equivalents marking off such a measure, there are found fewer than three semibreves, or the value thereof, then those semibreves that are altered have the value of eight minims; but if more than three are found in such a measure, then the semibreves that are altered have the value of only four minims, because this measure could not be completed otherwise. This is quite clear to anyone who has followed the foregoing carefully.

The fifteenth rule is this: a semibreve which is altered in *tempus novenarium* is always changed to the value of six minims; but in *tempus senarium* it is changed to the value of only four minims.

The sixteenth rule is this: an altered note can sometimes be imperfected by a preceding part but never by a following part because then a note would be altered unnecessarily since, if it were imperfected by a following part, even if it were by the next shorter value, a note would then be altered before a note shorter than itself, which is not necessary because there is no need to alter a note unless it precedes the next longer note. If it precedes a shorter, or a longer note which is not the next longer one, there is no need for alteration since such a note can be changed to the next longer value without any inconvenience, and therefore, etc.

The seventeenth rule is this: in *tempus quaternarium* every semibreve regularly notated always has the value of two minims, nor is any alteration ever made in this mensuration. The reason for this is that the *quaternaria* measure is complete without it.

The eighteenth rule is this: if in *modus maximarum perfectus*, between two *puncti* or their equivalents marking off such a measure, there are found three longs, whether as notes or rests, all are of equal value. And likewise, if in *modus longarum perfectus*, between two *puncti* or their equivalents marking off such a measure, there are found three breves, as notes or rests, all are of equal value. And likewise, if in *tempus perfectum*, between two *puncti* or their equivalents marking off such a measure, there are found three semibreves, as notes or rests, then all are of equal value. And the reason for all these things is that, since these perfections are already complete within the two *puncti* or their equivalents, there is clearly no reason why any one of the three notes [of these groups] specified should be greater or lesser in value than another, and therefore, etc.

The nineteenth rule is this: if in *modus maximarum imperfectus*, between two *puncti* or their equivalents marking off such a measure, there are found two longs, or the value thereof in notes or rests, then all are of equal value. And likewise, if in *modus longarum imperfectus*, between two *puncti* or their equivalents marking off such a measure, there are found two breves, or the value thereof in notes or rests, all the breves are of equal value. And likewise, if in *tempus imperfectum,* between two *puncti* or their equivalents marking off such a measure, there are found only two semibreves, or the value thereof in notes or rests, both these semibreves are of equal value. And the reason for all this is that, since these imperfections are already complete within the two *puncti* or their equivalents, there is clearly no reason why any one of the aforesaid notes should be greater or lesser in value than another [of the same kind], and therefore, etc.

The twentieth rule is this, and it applies to every mensuration in which an alteration can be made: whenever in any of these mensurations the notes shorter than the alterable note in a given measure are found to be of such number that they are insufficient, together with the alterable note or notes there, to complete the particular measure without an alteration of one or more of the alterable notes present, then one or more of those alterable notes must be altered, for the reason already mentioned several times above.

The twenty-first rule is this, and it is general like the twentieth: any semibreve that is altered can be changed by alteration only to the value of four or six or eight minims. This is quite obvious to anyone who considers it carefully.

The twenty-second rule is this: one and the same *punctus* can simultaneously mark both *modi,* that is, *maximarum* and *longarum,* and *tempus,* as shown in the following example, which I want to include all the perfections, i.e., of *modi* and *tempus.* In this example it is evident that the last *punctus* marks off all the measures, as anyone can see who studies it carefully. The example is this:[14]

[14] The example is interpreted according to Sartori's explanation (p. 128). Sartori observes that, strictly speaking, one *punctus* (i.e., the last) "marks off all the measures" only with regard to the second half of the example since two other *puncti* are used in the first half *(loc cit.).* Wolf, in his discussion of the equivalent example in the first redaction of the treatise (see Coussemaker III, p. 241), ignores what seems to be the point of the rule and its example, i.e., that a single *punctus* (here the last)

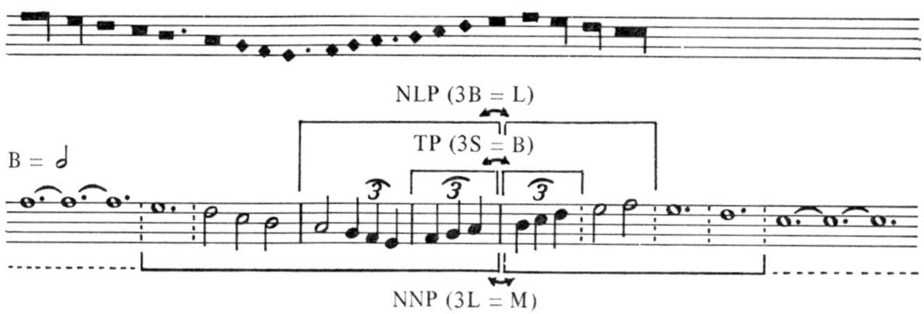


[Ligatures]

Now that we have covered the method of notating music in this practice in every mensuration without the use of ligatures, let us proceed to a discussion of ligatures themselves, treating concisely of the way notes are ligated and, for the sake of conciseness, omitting those things that are quite useless to this practice, handed down from some of the early writers — I mean propriety, opposite propriety, and perfection — because it is clear that they add little or nothing that is practically helpful.

I say, then, that a ligature is the joining *(coniunctio)* of certain notes to each other or their ligating *(ligatio)* by means of some *ligamentum*. To clarify this definition: you must know that there is a difference between a *ligamentum* on the one hand and a *cauda*, or *tractus*, which is the same thing, on the other. For a *ligamentum* is a line joining two notes, that is, starting from a note and ending in a note, thus:  , whereas a *cauda* or *tractus* is not a line joining two notes but one starting from a note and ending in space, thus:

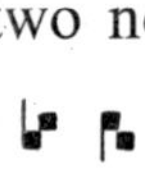

Moreover, it must be observed that there are two kinds of

can at times distinguish all the mensurations (the two *modi* plus *tempus*). He states (p. 218) that while the first *punctus* simultaneously marks a measure of NNI and NLP, the third delimits a measure of NLP and TP. In other words, he sees the first and third *puncti* as marking respectively the two *modi*, and one *modus* and a *tempus*.

ligature, ascending and descending. An ascending ligature is one in which the second note is higher than the first, thus:  , whereas a descending ligature is one in which the first note is higher than the second, thus: 

And notes are ligated in two ways, *recte* and *oblique*. *Recte*, thus:  *Oblique*, thus: 

So, having stated these facts, we must provide some rules for ligatures and, first, [rules] for the first note of a ligature, [of which] this rule [is first] and the first in our series: if the first note of a ligature has an ascending tail or stroke to the left, whether the ligature itself is ascending or descending, *recta* or *obliqua*, then the first two notes of the ligature will be semibreves; thus: 

The second rule is this: if a ligature is descending, whether *recta* or *obliqua*, and the first note of the ligature has a descending tail or stroke to the left, then the first note of the ligature will be a breve; thus:  [B, L]  [B, B]

The third rule is this: if a ligature is ascending, whether *recta* or *obliqua*, and the first note of the ligature lacks a stroke or tail, or has a descending one on the left, then the first note of the ligature will be a breve; thus:  [all B, B]

The fourth rule is this: if a ligature is descending and *obliqua* and the first note of the ligature lacks a stroke or tail, then the first note of the ligature will be a long; thus:  [L, B]

The fifth rule is this: if a ligature is descending and *recta* and the first note of the ligature lacks a stroke or tail, then the first note of the ligature will be either rectangular or square. If rectangular, the note is a *maxima*; thus:  [M, L]

But if a square, a long; thus:  [L, L]

The sixth rule is this: if a ligature is *recta* and ascending and the first note of the ligature has a descending tail or stroke to the right, then the first note of the ligature will be either rectangular or square. If rectangular, then the note is a *maxima*: thus: 

[M, B] But if square, a long; thus:  [L, B]

The following rules are for the last note in a ligature.

The first of these, and the seventh in our series, is this: if the last note of a ligature is ligated in an oblique manner, whether ascending or descending, it is always a breve, unless it happens to be the second note of a ligature in which the first has an ascending tail or stroke to the left: then it becomes a semibreve like the first note in order to complete a measure of the *tempus*. An example of the rule and its exception is this: 

The eighth rule is this: if the last note of a ligature is quadrangular and descending in respect to the penultimate note, whether the ligature itself is ascending or descending, then that last note of the ligature will be either rectangular or square. If rectangular, then the note is a *maxima*; thus:  [B, M]  [B, B, M]

But if a square, a long; thus:  [B, L]  [B, B, L]

And this rule holds good unless countered by the circumstance mentioned above; that is to say, in case the last note should be the second of two and the first should have an ascending tail or stroke on the left: then it becomes a semibreve like the first note, whatever its form may be, rectangular or square, in order to complete a measure of the *tempus*; thus: 

The ninth rule is this: if the last note of any ligature stands directly above or to the side of the penultimate note, and if it has a descending tail on the right, it will be a *maxima* if rectangular; thus:  [B, M] But if its form is square or slanting, it will be a long; thus:  [all B, L]
And again, this rule holds good unless countered by the circumstance mentioned now more than once. In that case the second note, whatever its form may be, goes with the first in order to complete a measure of the *tempus*, as we have said; thus: 

The tenth rule is this: if the last note of a ligature is ascending and it stands at the side of the penultimate note, provided it lacks a tail or stroke, it will be a breve regardless of its form; thus: , except for the circumstance mentioned now several times; thus: 

The following rule, and the eleventh in our series, concerns the intermediate notes, and it is this: all intermediate notes are breves unless the first note of the ligature has an ascending tail or stroke; in that case the second note becomes a semibreve like the first. An example of the rule and its exception is this:  [L, B, B, L]

 [B, B, B, B]  [S, S, B, L]  [S, S, B, L]
It follows from this rule that no *maxima* and no long should ever be included among the intermediate notes of a ligature.

The twelfth and last rule is this: if two longs are ligated in *modus maximarum perfectus*, thus:  , and likewise, if two breves are ligated in *modus longarum perfectus*, thus:  ; and likewise, if two semibreves are ligated in *tempus perfectum*, thus:  , the second note of these ligatures is always altered. However, if these notes are so ligated in imperfect measures, both notes of any such pair are of one and the same value. The reason for this is that, when these notes are ligated under the circumstances described, it is an indication that they are to complete a measure of the next longer note; and since this cannot be done in perfect measures without an alteration of the second note of these ligatures, it is rendered necessary that they be altered. But this does not happen in imperfect measures because the latter are complete without the alteration.

Now, as we have assigned no reasons for the above rules governing ligatures, except for the last, and in order, therefore, that you may have some explanation of the basis for both ligatures themselves and for mensural music in general, you should know that before the invention of mensural music people of early times had a certain manner of singing in plainchant which they were wont to call the "organic mode" *(modus organicus)* because they had derived it from the way organs were played (*...ipsum acceperant ab organorum pulsatione)*. This mode, then, meant that instead of giving all the notes in a chant equal value they would make some longer and others shorter according to the different groupings of the notes and according to differences in the ligatures, [e.g., whether they were] with stems or without stems; and mensural music originated from this variety. The various ligatures, differing in form and value, were combined with other things that pertain to mensural music.[15]

[15] Cf. Apel, p. 378.

[Syncopation]

Finishing our description of ligatures, let us proceed to a description of syncopation *(syncopa)*, which is the sweetest thing to be found in a piece of music and useful for what follows. Syncopation in music, then, is the division of a note into its parts with other notes placed between them, and these parts are related to each other *(ad invicem reduncuntur)* by reckoning the value of the divided note itself. Now, this musical syncopation originated as a counterpart or parallel of the syncope in grammer, because, just as in grammatical syncope a syllable — that is, the middle syllable or one of the intermediate syllables — is taken out of, or separated from, a word, so in this musical syncope one part of some note is separated from the other, or from the others. The only thing, then, that we have to note with regard to this musical syncopation is this: whenever any note-value divided by syncopation is completed after a number of longer notes, and cuts across the end of any measure of those longer notes, then at the point where that measure is completed, [i.e.,] at a subdivision of some one of those longer notes, above that note we need to place a *punctus* to show that the end of the measure is there. And this syncopation can be used in every mensuration. Here are examples of all these things.

[Rests]

With these few remarks on syncopation we move on to rests. And you should know, first, that a rest is a line intersecting a line or lines of the staff and indicating a cessation of sound. And it is of two kinds. A certain kind that is non-mensural *(sine mensura)* is called by several different names: unmeasured rest, general rest, common rest, and final rest; and it is notated with a line intersecting all the lines of the staff and occupying all its spaces, thus: 

The other is the mensural or measured rest, and it does not intersect all the lines of the staff or occupy all the spaces between the lines; thus: 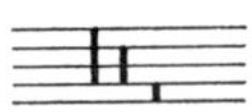 There are six rests of this kind corresponding to the six mensural notes used in this practice: a rest for the semiminim, a rest for the minim, a rest for the semibreve, a rest for the breve, a rest for the long, and a rest for the *maxima,* [although the last is] disregarded in practice as not necessary.

The rest for the semiminim has to be notated in two ways due to the fact that the semiminim also [has to be notated in two ways],[16] namely with an upward hook to the flag and without that hook. It begins on a line and ascends to the middle of the space, with a flag curved on top in the manner of semiminims; thus: 

The rest for the minim should also begin on a line and ascend to the middle of the space, but without a flag on top; thus: 
The rest for the semibreve should begin on a line and descend to

[16] "...secumdum quod et semiminima, scilicet..." etc. Both manuscripts have *et* here, which Sartori changes to *est*. See the introduction, p. 3.

the middle of the space, also without the flag; thus: 

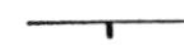

Now, the rests for the minim and the semiminim are notated with an ascending tail like the tail of the minim and semiminim [note-forms], but the semibreve rest is notated in descending fashion,

the reverse of the ascending tail just mentioned, and [thus these descending tails] produce rests for notes the reverse [of themselves],[17] in a sense. And in contrast to these rests, which are taken to the middle of the space, the rest for a breve must occupy a whole space;

thus: 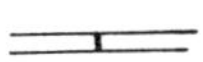

The rest for the long has to be notated in two ways, corresponding to the two different kinds of long; for just as the long sometimes has the value of two *tempora* and sometimes the value of three, so the rest for the long must sometimes have the value of two *tempora* and sometimes three. It has a value of two *tempora* when it occupies two spaces; thus: 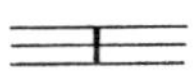 but it has the value of three *tempora* when it occupies three spaces; thus: 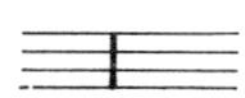 , because a rest is worth the same number of *tempora* as the spaces it occupies.

The rest for the *maxima*, though not used, has to be notated in several different ways, depending upon the number of *tempora* constituting its value. That is to say, just as a *maxima* has the value of four or six or nine *tempora* at various times, so it is possible to, write rests for this note that indicate these values; but since this can be done only by using a very much larger staff than is required in practice, rests for this note are in consequence disregarded. Here is an appropriate rule: a rest of more than three *tempora* should never be used because anything longer, if it is a mensural rest, cannot

[17] The translation represents an attempt to keep to the manuscript reading (see the introduction p. iii); but the whole Latin sentence is clumsy. Consider, e.g., the use of *producere* in two different senses (p. 66 in Sartori).

be notated on a five-line staff, which is sufficient for anything one needs to write, as is obvious to anybody who thinks about it carefully.

Secondly, you should know that rests can in no wise be imperfected or altered, because silence, which is their effect, can also in no wise be imperfected or altered, seeing that silence is nothing but a lack of sound, and a lack of sound can also in no wise be imperfected or altered, because a lack [of something] is in fact nothing since it is something which does not in fact exist.

Thirdly, you should know that the rest for a semibreve should never be used unless the value [in notes] equivalent to it has been completed in the measure in which it is included. Nor should the rest for a breve be used except after a complete *tempus*. Nor should the rest for a long be used except after a complete *modus longarum*.[18]

To understand the reason for this rule you must know that mensural rests were invented for two purposes, namely as musical ornaments and to provide nature with some relief from the fatigue of singing. Now, the rests for the minim and the semiminim were not invented principally to provide nature with relief from the fatigue of singing, since nature would obtain little relief therefrom. It is the other rests that were invented principally to provide nature with some relief from the fatigue of singing, though admittedly the rests for the minim and the semiminim are used too at times for this purpose, just as the other rests are also used at times as musical ornaments; but they were not invented principally for that purpose. With this preface, then, I say that anyone who should use the rests specified contrary to the conditions specified would at once incur an error, defeating the principal purpose for which rests were invented; for then nature would get no relief from the fatigue of singing but would, in fact, be burdened still more, as anyone who employs this practice can find out for himself—at least as regards the shorter values.

18 That is, the rests in question cannot be introduced in the middle of a value in notes equivalent to their own. See Sartori, pp. 139-141, where other sources for the rule are cited.

From this follows the rule so often quoted that a rest for a note of greater value should never be used between two shorter notes to make a syncopation, because to do so is at once to incur the error we are talking about, as anybody can see if he considers it carefully. And although this is so, there are some nevertheless who think to avoid this error in both the Italian and the French practice with this device: wanting to make a syncopation with a semibreve rest between two minims, they write rests of the *value* of a semibreve rest [instead], that is, rests for two or three minims; thus:  [19]

But this is wrong because, if you think carefully about it, they incur the afore-mentioned error as surely with this notion as if they wrote a rest worth a semibreve, for they burden nature as much with these two or three rests as they would with a single rest for the semibreve. And thus you know why it is that this rule must be understood to apply [either] to the use of a rest for a note of greater value or to the use of [several rests as] the equivalent of that value between two shorter notes in order to make a syncopation, [i.e.,] for the reason given above. And almost everyone using either the French or the Italian practice at the present time falls into this error, and falls into it totally while thinking to avoid it. There can also be another reason [for this rule, i.e.,] that, quite logically, any rest terminates the value of a note, at least [a rest] for the next longer [note].

Fourthly, and this follows from what has been said already, you must know that more than one rest should never be used where one would suffice for the purpose because this would be to create an unnecessary profusion, which is the greatest fault in art, as we have said.

Fifthly, you should know that the rest for an imperfect long, that is, a rest of two *tempora*, should never be used in *modus longarum perfectus*, nor should the rest for a perfect long, that is, a rest of three *tempora*, be used in *modus longarum imperfectus*; and likewise,

[19] In the manuscript the last note appears as a semibreve. See the introduction, p. 7.

the rest for an imperfect breve should never be used in *tempus perfectum*, nor should the rest for a perfect breve be used in *tempus imperfectum*. The reason for this is that rests must have the same value as their notes in the places where they are used; and since longs must be perfect by nature in *modus longarum perfectus* and imperfect in *modus longarum imperfectus*; and likewise, since breves must be perfect by nature in *tempus perfectum* and imperfect in *tempus imperfectum*, it follows that their rests must be in the same relation — which is the point we wanted to make clear. From this it follows that the rest for an imperfect semibreve should never be used in *senaria imperfecta* and *novenaria*, because semibreves in these mensurations are always perfect by nature. It also follows that [the rest] for a perfect semibreve should never be used in *senaria perfecta*, *quaternaria*, *octenaria*, and *duodenaria*, because semibreves in these mensurations are always imperfect by nature.[20]

[Diminution and augmentation]

Diminution and augmentation must now be considered, and both at the same time. There are, then, two kinds of diminution, for there is one kind which is something other than the replacement of a note by the next shorter one, and this is not the kind intended here. The other is the diminution which does consist of the re-

[20] Since no distinction in *form* is made between the perfect and imperfect breve rest and between the perfect and imperfect semibreve rest, as it is between the perfect and imperfect long rest, the extension of the prohibition to the two former means of course that these rests cannot be made to *function* as values other than the values they have "by nature." In his *Tractatus practicae de musica mensurabili* Prosdocimus sets forth the restrictions in the French system as follows (see Coussemaker III, p. 223 B): "It must be noted too that the rest for an imperfect semibreve should never be used in a piece in major prolation without an intrinsic or extrinsic sign. Likewise, a rest for an imperfect breve should never be used in a piece in *tempus perfectum* without an intrinsic or extrinsic sign. This is quite obvious to everybody and is conceded by everybody, because it is plainly not logical, in a piece in major prolation, where all semibreves are perfect by nature, and in a piece in *tempus perfectum*, where all breves are perfect by nature, that their rests should be imperfected without some indication [thereof], I say, whether they are rests for imperfect breves or imperfect semibreves."

placement of a note by the next shorter one, and this *is* the kind intended here. Consequently it is defined as follows: diminution is the replacement of a note by the next shorter one. Likewise, I say in regard to augmentation that there are two kinds of augmentation, for there is one kind of augmentation which is something other than the replacement of a note by the next longer one, and this is not the kind intended here. The other is the augmentation which does consist of the replacement of a note by the next longer one, and this *is* the kind intended here. Consequently it is defined as follows: augmentation is the replacement of a note by the next longer one.

Now, the reason why this augmentation and diminution were needed is that they enable us to make discants of notable length over a short tenor [which can then be] repeated several times in different ways without a monotonous reiteration of time values *(sine prolongatione figurationis)* in that tenor.[21] Therefore, contemporary musicians are much in error, both those who follow the Italian practice and those who follow the French, when they use this augmentation and diminution not only in tenors [to be] repeated several times in different ways but also in tenors not repeated several times; and not only in tenors but even in discants. Nor is this necessary, because they could just as well notate their parts in regular notation and avoid monotonous reiteration of time values in those parts as they can by using augmentation and diminution.

The rules for this augmentation and diminution are the two following:

The first is this: in the diminution we are talking about here, a *maxima* is replaced by a long, a long by a breve, a breve by a semibreve, a semibreve by a minim, and a minim by the semiminim which is sung in duple proportion to the minim. Likewise, I say that in the augmentation we are talking about here, the semiminim which is sung in duple proportion to the minim is replaced by the minim, a minim

[21] See Sartori, p. 142.

by a semibreve, a semibreve by a breve, a breve by a long, and a long by a *maxima.*

The second rule is this: in this kind of augmentation and diminution a perfect note is replaced by another perfect note, an imperfect note by another imperfect note, an altered note by another altered note, and an unaltered note by another unaltered note — with this proviso, that the notes which replace the others are capable of being perfected or imperfected or altered.

Note, too, that these rules must be understood to apply to rests as well as to their notes.

[*Color* and *talea*]

Now there follows a discussion of *color* or *talea*, both meaning the same thing. *Color* or *talea* in music, then, consists of several repetitions of the same [series of] note-values or pitches in a piece of music, with nothing in between [the repetitions]. You can gather from this definition that there are two kinds of *color* or *talea*, one in which only the same note-values are repeated and one in which only the same pitches are repeated. But a third can be added, in which both the identical note-values and the identical pitches are repeated at the same time. You must know, therefore, that the two names *color* and *talea* mean one and the same thing and that there is no difference between them except the names. They may be compared in this respect to the two names *father* and *priest (presbiter, sacerdos)*: just as these two names, father and priest, are applied to one and the same thing, though with different connotations — *father* connoting "he who shows the way" [*presbiter* from *prebens iter*] and *priest*, "he who gives the sacraments" [*sacerdos* from *dans sacra*][22] —

[22] The author's etymology is of course faulty in the first instance, *presbiter* being Greek for "elder"( πρεσβύτερος ). The mistake is apparently occasioned, at least in part, by the loss of ending (-os = us) and the replacement of y with i as a transliteration of *upsilon.*

so the two different names *color* and *talea* can be applied to one and the same thing, though with different connotations: *color* is used metaphorically for the "color", meaning repetition, found in rhetoric, and the metaphor comes about in this way, that just as rhetorical color is produced by several repetitions of the same statement, so musical color is produced by several repetitions of the same pitches or note-values. On the other hand, the term *talea* is applied in this context because repetitions of this sort are so arranged that each repetition is separate or distinct *(taleata sive divisa)* from another. And although this is [theoretically] correct, still there is common agreement among all musicians to apply the term *color* only to repetitions of the same pitches and *talea* only to repetitions of the same note-values — always without anything more between one *talea* and the next or between one *color* and the next.

From all that has been said, then, from the beginning up to this point, you can gather how much the Italian practice differs from the French, and how much validity there is in each, and which is the more worthy of esteem. And it should be apparent by now that this Italian practice is by no means so defective as many claim[23] who look into it but superficially and say that whereas any Italian piece can be notated in the French manner, the reverse is not true, i.e., that not every French piece can be notated in the Italian manner. I affirm the opposite of this statement: I say that whereas any French piece, correctly and properly notated with the elements of notation *(figurationes)* that are legitimate in French practice, can be notated in the Italian manner, the reverse is not true, i.e., that not every Italian piece, correctly and properly notated with the elements of notation that are legitimate in Italian practice, can be notated in the French manner. To deliver myself of this matter briefly and to the point, I say that any Italian piece that is in *octenaria* or *duodenaria* throughout can never be notated according to French practice in such a way as to be sung as it is supposed to be, that is, in *sesquitertia*

[23] A paraphrase of the first clause of what begins as a conditional sentence: "And if this Italian practice is as defective as many claim..." ("Et si haec ars ytalica ita defectuosa sit uti asserunt multi..."). In the course of a long and rambling extension of this protasis, the author loses his way and never arrives at the apodosis. Lapses of this sort are not characteristic of Prosdocimus.

*proportio*. And anyone can see this who has a thorough understanding of the proper and legitimate elements of notation in each practice, the French and the Italian. Thus, in the case of an *octenaria* or *duodenaria* piece in which there would be found only minims and semibreves of the value of two minims, such that no two of those semibreves would be found on the same line or space, it is obvious that this could not be notated in the French manner except by means of [special] signs placed at the beginning of the piece to show us this *sesquitertia proportio*. But clearly this notation is quite extrinsic to the French practice; worse, it is downright irrational, because it would make the notes in such a piece proportional to other notes not present in the same piece; and this is plainly a great absurdity of the French practice, for any note that is sung in proportion to another should be sung in proportion to some other note present in the same piece, as would not be the case with the notation we are considering.[24]

Now to end this treatise, I must tell you — in the event you may be feeling somewhat puzzled — that in this latest version *(ultima... corectione)* of it I have changed certain things which, as a consequence of further acquaintance with this practice, seemed to me should be changed. And these [innovations], which are somewhat at variance with the Italian notation in current use, I have taken from the *Pomerium* of Marchettus of Padua. However, if you prefer the Italian notation in current use, go back to my first treatise on the Italian practise, the one I wrote before this, and there you will find your purpose answered.

So then, let this be the end of the treatise compiled by the least of musicians, Prosdocimus de Beldemandis, Paduan, in the town of Montagnana, District of Padua, A. D. 1412, to the glory and honor

[24] Strictly speaking, of course, the values in the hypothetical piece considered here would not be performed in *proportio sesquitertia* to other values in the same piece regardless of which notational system were used, since it has been stipulated that the only values present are to be minims and semiminims (of the value of ½ Mi). *Proportio sesquitertia* in this situation, then, describes the relation of the values actually present in the piece to the basic reference value (i.e., the so-called "integer valor"; see, e.g., Apel, pp. 188 ff. *et alibi*). The point, in short, is that *octenaria* and *duodenaria* provide particular *tempos* not intrinsically available from the French system.

of Almighty God and the Church Triumphant. Amen.

Here ends a treatise on the practice of mensural music in the Italian manner, compiled by Prosdocimus of Padua.